# The MAILBOX®

The Education Center®

# Simply Seasonal ABCs

grades PreK-K

W9-ABB-100

**FALL/WINTER**

## Thematic Literacy Units to Build and Strengthen

- **Phonemic Awareness**
- **Phonological Awareness**
- **Phonics**
- **Alphabet Skills**

and Other Early Literacy Skills

**Managing Editor:** Cindy K. Daoust

**Editorial Team:** Becky S. Andrews, Kimberley Bruck, Karen P. Shelton, Diane Badden, Thad H. McLaurin, Sharon Murphy, Kimberly A. Murphy, Gerri Primak, Leanne Stratton, Allison E. Ward, Karen A. Brudnak, Sarah Hamblet, Hope Rodgers, Dorothy C. McKinney, Janet Boyce, Beth Marquardt

**Production Team:** Lisa K. Pitts, Pam Crane, Rebecca Saunders, Jennifer Tipton Cappoen, Chris Curry, Sarah Foreman, Theresa Lewis Goode, Ivy L. Koonce, Clint Moore, Greg D. Rieves, Barry Slate, Donna K. Teal, Tazmen Carlisle, Amy Kirtley-Hill, Kristy Parton, Cathy Edwards Simrell, Lynette Dickerson, Mark Rainey, Cathy Spangler Bruce, Kimberly Richard

www.themailbox.com

# Table of Contents

Manufactured in the United States
10  9  8  7  6  5  4  3  2

# How to Use

1. **Select a topic.**
2. **Choose ideas to enhance your lesson plans.**
3. **Use the timesaving reproducibles to strengthen early literacy skills.**

## Quickly assemble the literacy booklets.

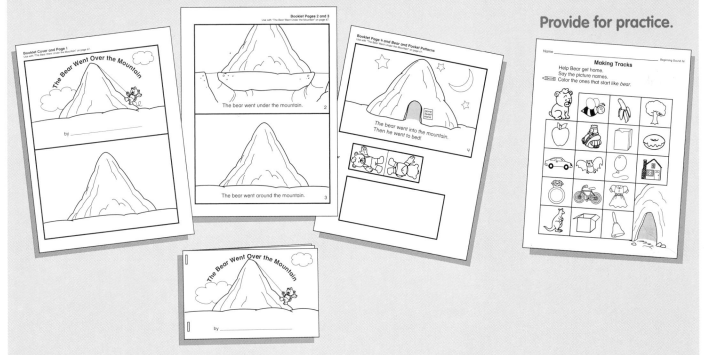

## Provide for practice.

## Adapt the open pages to match students' abilities and skills.

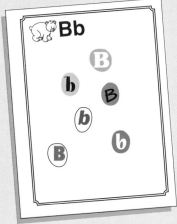

Letter Recognition

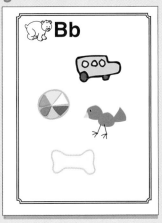

Sound Association

Letter-Sound Association

### Apple Art
*Associating A with the short A sound*

This "apple-rific" display is sure to help your little ones make letter-sound connections! Collect a fast-food drink tray for every four students. Cut each tray into four sections and trim each section to resemble an apple, leaving a cardboard stem as shown. Place the prepared apples in a center with red and brown washable tempera paint. Invite each child to visit the center and paint an apple red and the stem brown, softly repeating the short *A* sound while she works. When the paint is dry, help each child personalize a green construction paper leaf and tape it to the stem. Then help her use a permanent marker to write a lowercase *A* in the center of her apple. If desired, showcase the apples on a bulletin board for an "a-a-absolutely" fabulous display!

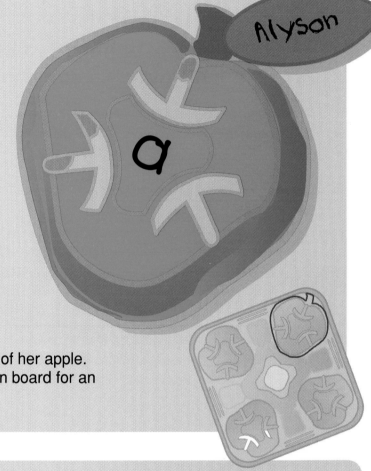

**Falling Apples Song**
*(sung to the tune of "Short'nin' Bread")*

Apples are falling, falling, falling.
Apples are falling off the tree.
Apples are falling, falling, falling.
Crisscross applesauce—all sit down!

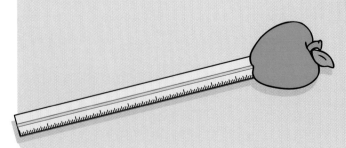

### Falling Apples
*Tracking print, recognizing words*

Get youngsters on the right track with this catchy tune! To prepare, copy the song shown on a chart, leaving plenty of space between words. Then make an apple pointer by taping an apple cutout to the end of a ruler. Teach youngsters the song, tracking each word with the pointer as you go. Invite volunteers to take turns tracking the print as the class slowly sings the song several times. Then challenge different volunteers to use the pointer to identify specific words, such as *are, the,* and *tree.* Later, put the chart and pointer in a center for individual practice.

## Applesauce As

Help your little ones develop a taste for writing! Place a large spoonful of apple-sauce on a small foam plate for each child. Have each child use a plastic spoon to spread the applesauce on his plate. Then invite him to use the spoon to write an uppercase *A* in the applesauce. When he's finished, direct him to "erase" the letter by spreading the applesauce again. Next, have him write and erase a lowercase *A* in the same manner. Then have him write additional letters as desired. Complete the activity by encouraging students to eat their applesauce. Fun!

## Apple-o

*Understanding that words are made up of letters*

Any time is a great time to sing this cute adaptation of the traditional bingo song! After teaching young-sters the words, have them sing the song once. When the letters in the word *apple* are sung, have students substitute a clap while silently mouthing the letter *A*. Then have them sing the remaining letters and finish the verse as usual. Continue in this manner, clapping and mouthing each letter, in turn, until all the letters have been replaced with claps.

*(sung to the tune of "Bingo")*

There was a tree that grew a fruit,
And apple was its name-o.
A-p-p-l-e, a-p-p-l-e, a-p-p-l-e—
And apple was its name-o.

## A-p-p-l-e

*Writing one's name*

How many letters are in the word *apple?* Five, of course! Youngsters will enjoy counting the letters in their names with this creative activity. Draw a simple tree outline on a sheet of paper; then make a copy for each child. Help each child color the tree and then write his name below it. Next, have him count the letters in his name. Direct him to use a red bingo dauber to print one apple on the tree for each letter in his name. When the ink dries, help him use a permanent marker to write one letter on each apple. Display the trees for an orchard of letters!

## Apple Pie, Please!

*Reading illustrated directions*

After a reading of Zoe Hall's *The Apple Pie Tree,* try an easy reading activity that your little ones can really sink their teeth into! In advance, copy page 10 and set it aside for later use. Then cut out the recipe cards on page 9 and laminate them for durability. Place the cards at a center with the ingredients and utensils shown. Show your little chefs the recipe cards and enlist their help in reading aloud the cards. Discuss the pictures that show how to make apple pie. Then arrange the cards in order and help each child read and follow the directions to make a personal apple pie. Yum!

Add crust. 1

Add apples. 2

Add topping. 3

Apple pie! 4

**Ingredients for one:**
vanilla wafer
2 tbsp. canned apple pie filling
1 tsp. granola

**Utensils and supplies:**
foil cupcake liner for each student
tablespoon
teaspoon
plastic spoon for each student

## Picked Fresh
*Adding onsets to rimes*

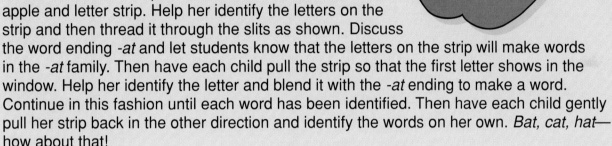

Pick a bumper crop of fresh new words! In advance, make a red construction paper copy of page 8 for each child in a small group. Use a craft knife to cut slits where indicated on each apple. Then distribute the copies. Have each child cut out her apple and letter strip. Help her identify the letters on the strip and then thread it through the slits as shown. Discuss the word ending *-at* and let students know that the letters on the strip will make words in the *-at* family. Then have each child pull the strip so that the first letter shows in the window. Help her identify the letter and blend it with the *-at* ending to make a word. Continue in this fashion until each word has been identified. Then have each child gently pull her strip back in the other direction and identify the words on her own. *Bat, cat, hat*—how about that!

## It's Apple Time!
*Matching pictures to text*

Fall is prime apple-picking time, but how does an apple tree look in spring and summer? Find out with this adorable accordion booklet! In advance, make a class supply of pages 10 and 11. Help each child cut out the pages along the heavy lines and then glue them together where indicated. When the glue is dry, accordion-fold each child's booklet. Read the booklet together and discuss what season each page describes. Next, have each child follow the directions shown to decorate the pages and then color and personalize the booklet cover. When a child's booklet is complete, encourage him to take it home to read with a family member.

Page 1: Color the treetop light green. Color the trunk brown. Glue on pink tissue paper apple blossoms.

Page 2: Color the treetop green. Color the trunk brown. Press a pinky fingertip on a washable green stamp pad; then print small green apples on the tree.

Page 3: Color the treetop green. Color the trunk brown. Press an index fingertip on a washable red stamp pad; then print ripe red apples on and near the tree.

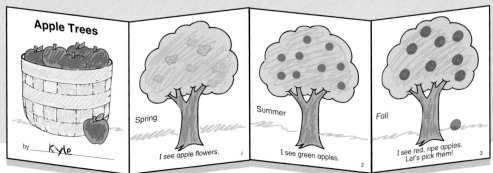

# Apple Pattern and Letter Strip

Use with "Picked Fresh" on page 7.

at

_____
name

s r p m h f c b

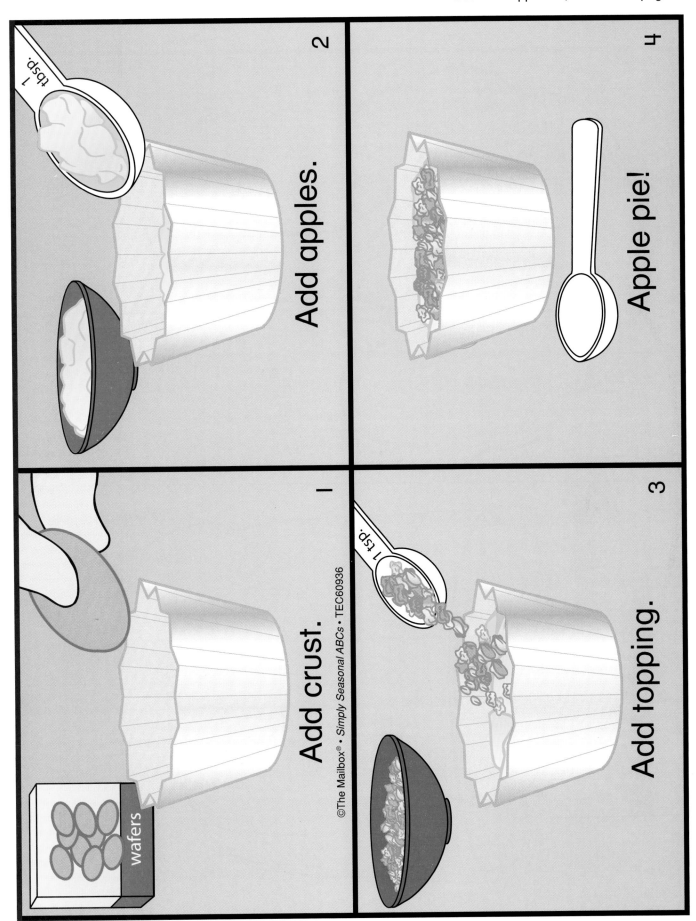

2 Add apples.

4 Apple pie!

1 Add crust.

wafers

3 Add topping.

1 tsp.

1 tbsp.

©The Mailbox® • *Simply Seasonal ABCs* • TEC60936

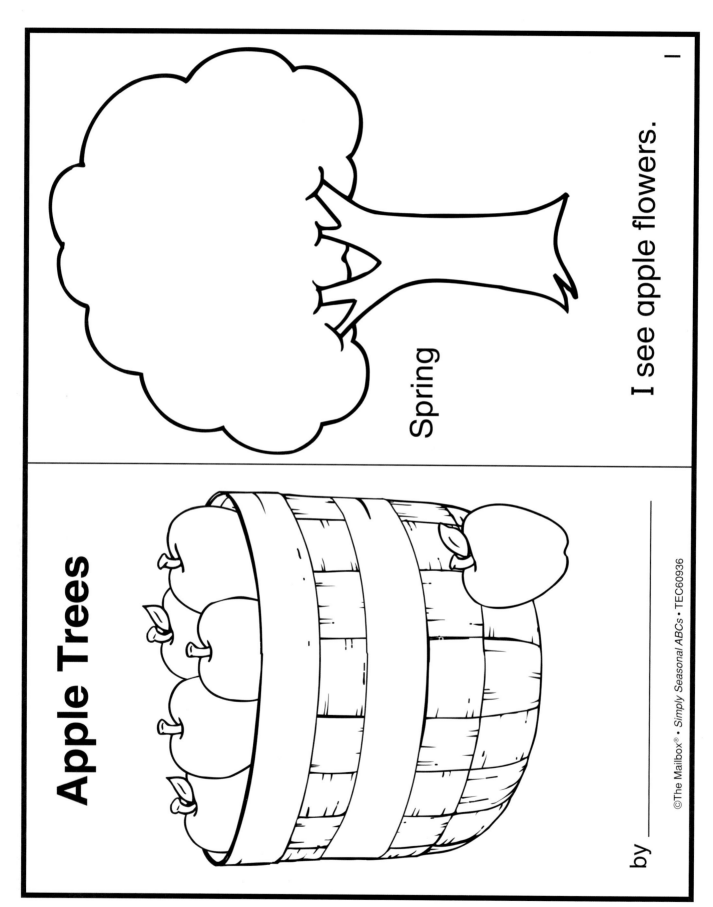

I

Spring

I see apple flowers.

Apple Trees

by _____

©The Mailbox® • *Simply Seasonal ABCs* • TEC60936

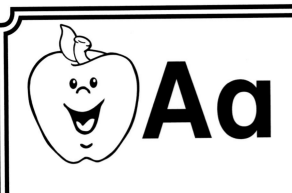 # Aa

# L Is for Leaf!

## Leaf Leaping

*Recognizing initial sound /l/*

Leaping little ones! This outdoor letter-sound activity is sure to get your youngsters moving! Take students outside and give each student a piece of chalk to use to draw a large leaf shape on a sidewalk or paved surface. Collect the chalk and direct each student to stand outside of her leaf. Announce a variety of words, one at a time, including some that start with *L* and some that do not. Have students compare each word's beginning sound to that of the word *leaf.* If the word starts like *leaf,* the youngsters should leap onto their leaves. If the word does not, they should stand still. After each word, observe youngsters' actions to check for accuracy. No doubt, your little leapers will fall for this activity!

## "Unbe-leaf-able" Letter *L*

*Associating L with /l/*

Youngsters will ooh and aah over this impressive letter *L* display! Cut out a large uppercase and lowercase *L* from poster board. Provide each youngster with one large and one small colorful leaf cutout (patterns on page 18). Then invite each student to decorate her leaves using glitter glue and markers. After the glue dries, direct her to glue her large leaf on the uppercase *L* and her small leaf on the lowercase *L.* As she does this, have her say, "*L* is for *leaf,*" emphasizing the /l/ sound in *leaf.* Display these lavish, leafy *L*s for all to see!

**pumpkin pointer**

**pocket**

# Pumpkins

## Oh, I wish I were a pumpkin,

## A pumpkin, a pumpkin.

## Oh, I wish I were a pumpkin,

## So orange, big, and fat.

# A Patch of Pumpkins

Cut. Match. Glue.

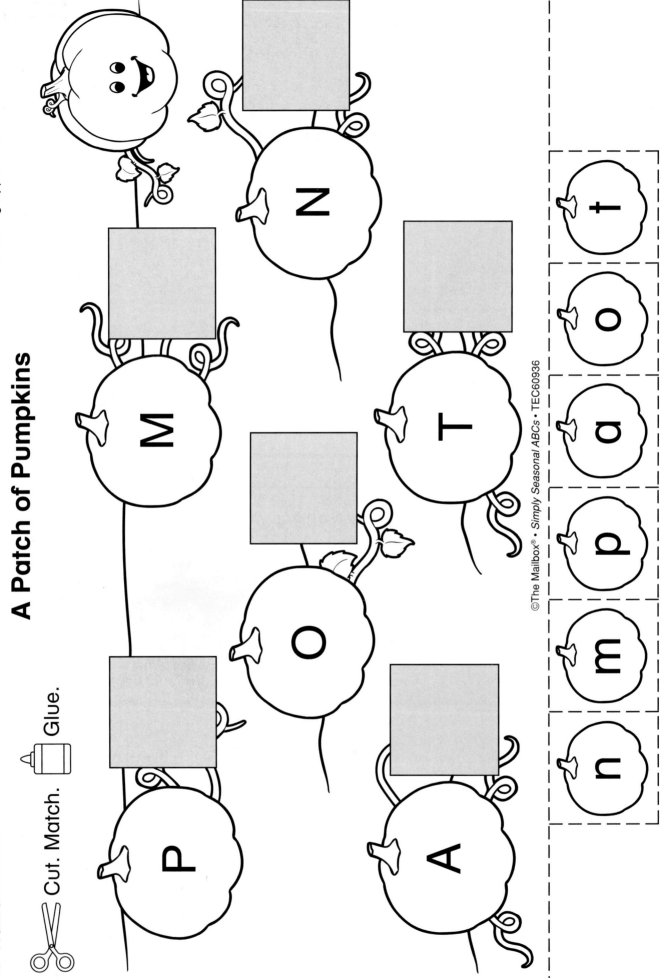

©The Mailbox® • *Simply Seasonal ABCs* • TEC60936

# Pp

## Ferris Wheel Fun

### Recognizing initial sound /f/

This classroom Ferris wheel display provides youngsters with fabulous initial /f/ practice. Gather a variety of magazine picture cutouts, some that start with *F* and some that do not. Draw a simple Ferris wheel, like the one shown, on a large sheet of bulletin board paper and post it on a wall or bulletin board. Give each child a Ferris wheel seat cutout (page 38) and direct her to color it as desired. Next, have her glue it to a 6" x 9" sheet of construction paper. Invite each child to look through the magazine cutouts and choose one that begins with *F*. Then have her glue it on the construction paper above the seat as shown. Next, help her trim around the seat and magazine cutout. Display each completed seat on the Ferris wheel display. Encourage youngsters to visit the Ferris wheel display and name each picture, emphasizing the /f/ sound. What f-f-fun!

## Going to the Fair

### Using speaking and listening skills

Come one, come all to this circle-time game! Read aloud a book about a fair, such as *Night at the Fair* by Donald Crews. After reading, encourage youngsters to name different items available at a fair, such as tickets, pizza, lemonade, ice cream, cotton candy, or peanuts. Begin the game by reciting, "I'm going to the fair, and I want to buy peanuts." Then invite a student to repeat the sentence, substituting a different item for *peanuts*. Encourage each youngster to listen carefully, making sure not to repeat an item that has already been said. Continue the game until each student has had a turn. There certainly is a lot to buy at a fair!

## Just Ducky Letters
*Identifying letters*

Invite youngsters to step right up and play this letter identification game! In advance, obtain a supply of plastic ducks. Use a permanent marker to write a different letter on the bottom of each duck. Float the ducks in your water table or a large container partially filled with water. Invite a student to remove a duck and name the letter on its underside. Check for accuracy and then direct her to place the duck back in the water. (Have more advanced students name the letter and its sound.) Continue in this manner until every student has had a turn. This letter game is just ducky!

## Prize Pie Rhymes
*Matching rhymes*

Rhyming practice is as easy as pie at this center! To prepare, gather four nine-inch pie tins and label each with a different one of the following rimes: *-an, -at, -ee, -op.* Cut four seven-inch construction paper circles into quarters. Decorate each quarter to look like a piece of pie. Copy the rhyming cards on page 39; then color them and cut them out. Glue each card to a separate pie piece; then laminate the pie pieces if desired. Store the pie pieces in a resealable plastic bag and place the bag at a center along with the pie tins. Instruct each center visitor to remove one pie piece at a time and name the picture. Then have him place the pie piece in the corresponding pie tin. Have him continue in this manner until all four pies are complete. For an added treat, reward each of your little pie makers with a real piece of pie!

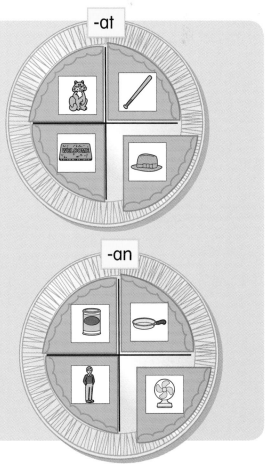

35

## Popcorn Sort

Sorting uppercase and lowercase letters

There's no need to wait in line at this popcorn-themed center! Obtain two clean and empty popcorn tubs or boxes. Make several popcorn cutouts similar to the ones shown. Program each cutout with a different uppercase or lowercase letter. Store the programmed cutouts in a resealable plastic bag and place the bag at a center along with the popcorn tubs. Invite a center visitor to sort the uppercase letters into one tub and the lowercase letters into the other tub. Vary the center by programming additional cutouts with clip art and having students sort them by rhymes.

## Basket Toss

*Identifying and sorting initial sounds*

Here's a fun small-group game that helps youngsters practice sorting initial letter sounds! Gather two laundry baskets and a supply of Ping-Pong or foam balls. Enlarge two picture cards from page 39 that represent words with different initial sounds that you want students to practice. Color the pictures and tape each card to a different basket. Use a permanent marker to program each ball with one of the two initial letters from the chosen picture cards. Store the balls in a large container and place the container in an open area of the classroom along with the laundry baskets. Have each student line up and, in turn, remove a ball from the container. Then have him identify the letter and its sound. Next, direct him to name the picture on each basket and toss the ball into the basket with the matching sound. Check for accuracy and continue the activity until each youngster has had a turn. Little ones are sure to have a ball sorting letters!

## Child Pattern
Use with "Trick-or-Treat Tune" on page 46.

## Candy Cards
Use with "Monster Munch" on page 45.

©The Mailbox® • *Simply Seasonal ABCs* • TEC60936

Use with "A Dreadful Dwelling" on page 46.

hanging spider 1

happy bat 2

hooting owl 3

hairy cat 4

Happy
Halloween! 5

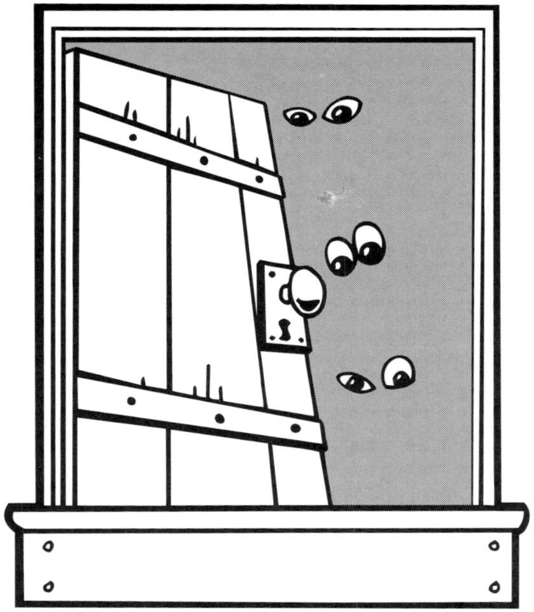

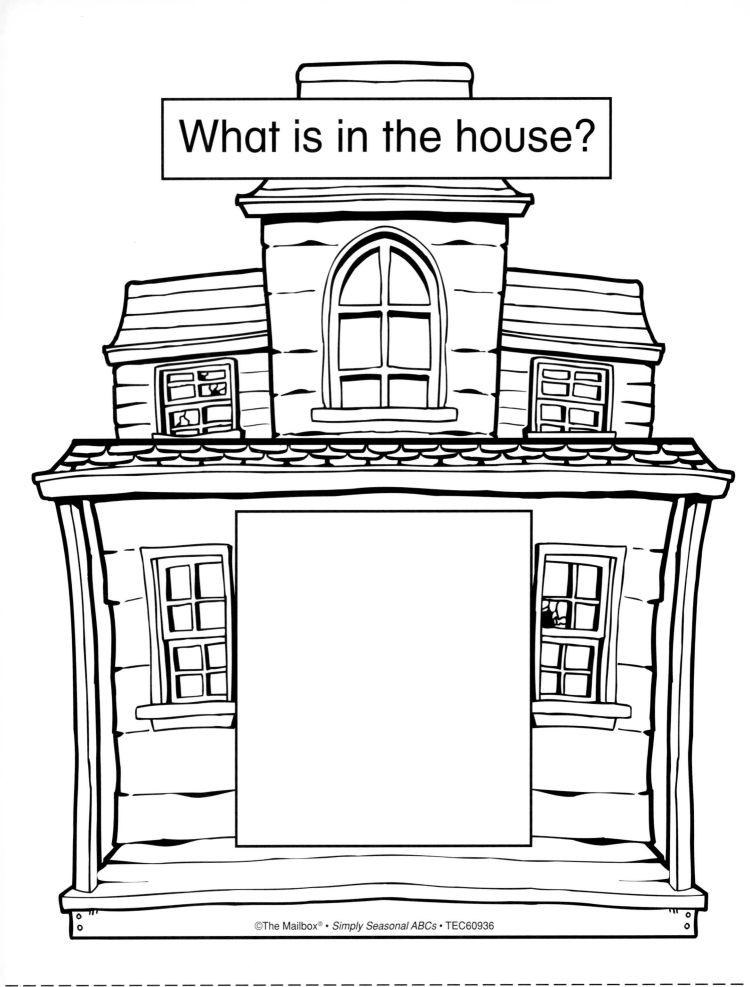

# What is in the house?

**Note to the teacher:** Use with "A Dreadful Dwelling" on page 46.

# Hh

# T Is for Turkey!

## Talking Turkey

### Recognizing initial sound /t/

Youngsters become fluent in turkey talk when they identify the sound of the letter *T* with these cute puppets! Instruct each child to brush orange, red, and yellow paint on the palm and four fingers of his nondominant hand. Then help him press his hand on a sheet of tan construction paper. Also have him paint a wooden ice-cream spoon brown. When the handprints and spoons are dry, help each youngster cut out his print. Encourage him to use a fine-tip permanent marker to draw a turkey face on the spoon. Next, have him glue the spoon to the front of the print. Then have him glue a jumbo craft stick to the back of the print to make a puppet. When the glue is dry, invite each student to come to your large-group area with his puppet in hand. Say a common word. If the word begins with /t/ like *turkey*, prompt each child to raise his turkey puppet and gobble. If the word does not begin with /t/, have each student sit quietly. That's terrific!

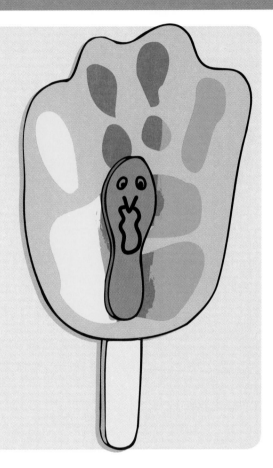

(sung to the tune of "Short'nin' Bread")

We are having ![turkey], ![turkey], ![turkey].
We are having ![turkey] on Thanksgiving Day.
We are having ![turkey], ![turkey], ![turkey].
We are having ![turkey] on Thanksgiving Day.
Not having chicken, not having fish.
Just having ![turkey], as much as you wish.
Bring out the food; bring out each dish.
Bring out the ![turkey], as much as you wish.
We are having ![turkey], ![turkey], ![turkey].
We are having ![turkey] on Thanksgiving Day.

## A Turkey Tune

### Developing concepts of print

What is a traditional food some people eat for Thanksgiving? Why, turkey, of course! Youngsters celebrate this dish—and practice concepts of print—with a nifty rebus song. Use the turkey cards on page 58 to make rebus song lyrics on a sheet of chart paper as shown. Post the lyrics in your large-group area. Invite a volunteer to point to the words to indicate where you should begin reading. Encourage students to help you read through the lyrics as you follow each line with your finger. Then lead students in singing the song.

## Following Fowl

**Matching uppercase and lowercase letters**

Turkeys in the sand table? Youngsters are sure to ponder the possibility when they see this collection of turkey tracks! Use the pattern on page 58 to make ten brown construction paper turkey tracks. Label each of five tracks with a capital letter. Label each remaining track with a matching lowercase letter. Place the tracks at your sand table. Encourage each youngster to match the uppercase and lowercase letters and place the matching tracks together in the sand. No doubt quite a few turkeys have been walking through this sand!

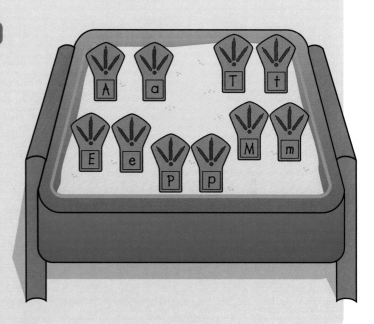

## Barnyard Banter

**Making connections between spoken words and print**

Youngsters think about words that represent sounds with this unique rhyme and activity! Lead youngsters in reciting the rhyme shown below. Explain that many of the sounds animals make can be written down as words. Then write the word *gobble* on a sheet of chart paper and read the word aloud. Encourage students to name sounds that other animals make as you write their ideas on the chart paper. Squeak, roar, meow!

gobble
moo
woof
tweet
squeak
meow
cluck
roar
oink

"Gobble, gobble," says the turkey,
Not "moo," "woof," or "tweet."
Nor will it say, "How do you do?"
To an animal it might meet.
But it's just fine with me
If it makes a gobbling sound.
Because gobbling makes me giggle.
It's the silliest sound around!

## Turkey Tale

Youngsters will be very thankful for this cute little rhyming booklet! For each child, make a copy of the booklet pages (pages 59 and 60) and a copy of the turkey body (page 61). Encourage each student to color and cut out the booklet pages. Help him stack the pages in order and then staple them between two brown construction paper covers. Have each child color the turkey body and then glue it to the front cover. Help him write the title shown and his name. Then invite him to glue colorful construction paper strips to the back cover to resemble feathers. Allow time for the glue to dry. Read aloud the booklet several times. When youngsters are familiar with the words, invite them to name the rhyming words. *Mat* rhymes with *hat!*

"A TuRkey Tale"
Alex

## A Guest for Dinner

*Writing to complete a prompt*

This writing idea puts a whole new spin on the phrase "a turkey dinner!" Give each youngster a sheet of paper programmed with the prompt shown. Read the prompt aloud. Then encourage each student to write (or dictate as you write) a type of food in the space provided. Then have her draw a picture to match the writing. That turkey is stuffed!

If a turkey came for dinner, it would think it's great
To have some ___spgete___ on its plate!

56

## Fancy Feathers
### *Identifying beginning sounds*

Students will flock to this center to supply a turkey with oodles of fancy feathers! Cut out a copy of the turkey body and picture cards on page 61. Color the turkey, label it with the letter *T,* and glue it to a brown construction paper circle. Glue each picture card to a colorful feather cutout. Laminate the prepared props if desired. Then place them at a center. A child visits the center and chooses a feather. She says the name of the picture and identifies the initial consonant. If the picture's name begins with /t/, she places the feather above the turkey. If it doesn't begin with /t/, she places it in a separate pile. She continues in the same way for each feather. What a lovely gobbler!

## Lurkey, Nurkey, Zurkey!
### *Substituting beginning sounds*

Your little ones won't gobble during this letter substitution activity, but they just might giggle! Make a class supply of consonant cards, making sure there are several *T*s. Label a sheet of paper with the word *turkey,* omitting the letter *T.* Post the paper in your large-group area. To begin, explain that the first letter in the word *turkey* is missing. Have a child choose a card. Encourage students to identify the letter and its sound. Then invite the child to hold his card against the chart paper as if it's the first letter in the word. Prompt students to help you read the resulting word and then decide whether the letter is correct. Continue in the same way with each remaining card. Now that sounds like fun!

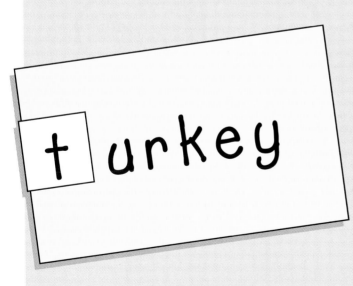

# Turkey Cards

Use with "A Turkey Tune" on page 54.

# Turkey Track Patterns

Use with "Following Fowl" on page 55.

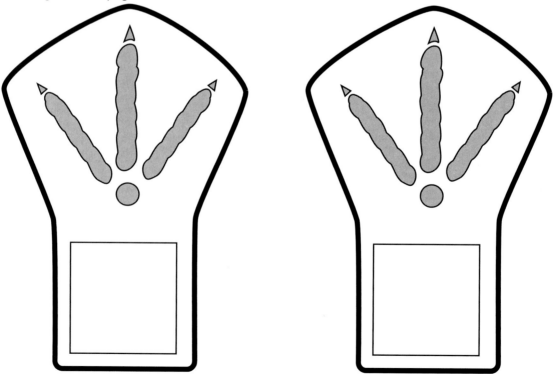

2

Turkey at the fair.

4

Turkey with a mouse.

1

Turkey in a chair.

©The Mailbox® • *Simply Seasonal ABCs* • TEC60936

3

Turkey in a house.

# Booklet Pages
Use with "Turkey Tale" on page 56.

6

Turkey with a hat.

8

Turkey in a bed.

5

Turkey on a mat.

Welcome

7

Turkey on a sled.

# Turkey Body Pattern

Use with "Turkey Tale" on page 56 and "Fancy Feathers" on page 57.

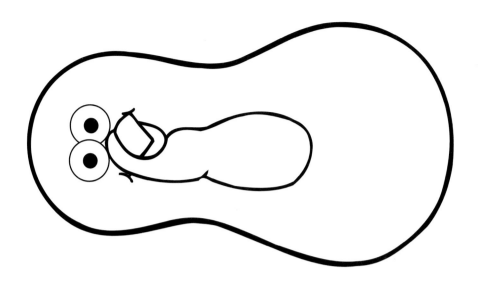

## Picture Cards

Use with "Fancy Feathers" on page 57.

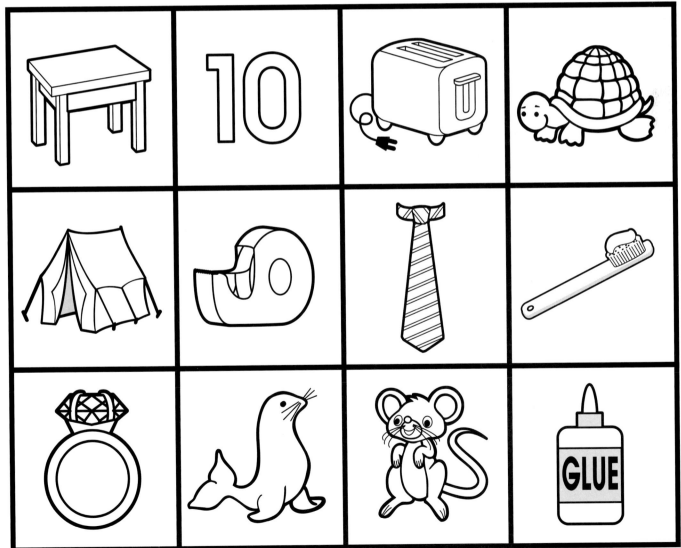

# Turkey Tips

 Color.  Cut.

Glue cards that show the letter *T* or *t*.

T  S  t  t  A  t

t  T  T

# Tt

# B Is for Bear!

## Bear Wear

*Developing awareness of the /b/ sound*

These adorable bear hats are just the thing to get your little ones thinking about the /b/ sound! To prepare, cut the centers from a class supply of paper plates, leaving two ears as shown. Point out that the word *bear* begins with the letter *B;* then encourage little ones to listen for the /b/ sound as they repeat the word. Invite each child to color a prepared plate brown or black to resemble a bear's fur and ears. While students work, encourage them to softly repeat the /b/ sound. When the hats are complete, invite youngsters to don them and pretend to be bears crawling, stomping, and looking for honey in your classroom. It's fun to be a bear!

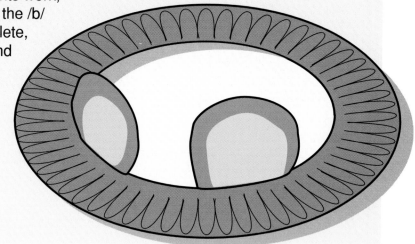

## Sounds Like a Bear!

*Recognizing initial sound /b/*

Invite your little ones to listen for words that begin with /b/ in this "bear-y" fun variation of Simon Says! Review the /b/ sound. If desired, have youngsters wear the bear hats made in "Bear Wear" above. Explain that when you say a word that begins like *bear,* each child should roar like a bear. If they hear a word that starts with a different sound, they should sit quietly. Then slowly say words that begin with /b/ and words that begin with other sounds while checking for understanding. After several rounds, choose a volunteer to lead the game. Oh boy—*bear* starts with /b/!

## Bear's Basket

*Associating the letter B with the sound /b/*

Would a bear enjoy eating foods that begin with the letter *B?* You bet! Show students a picnic basket and a stuffed bear, and explain that the bear wants a picnic of foods whose names begin with *B*. Have youngsters suggest foods as you write them on a chart, making sure to highlight the beginning letter *B* in each. Then reread the words, emphasizing the /b/ sound in each. Next, put the basket in your dramatic-play center with a variety of play foods and clean, empty packages for foods whose names begin with letter *B*. Prompt students visiting this center to name each food while packing a letter *B* picnic. Mmm—bears like beans, bananas, and bagels!

### B Foods

| | |
|---|---|
| beans | hotdog buns |
| butter | berries |
| bananas | burgers |
| bread | bagels |

## Rhyme Time

*Recognizing rhyming words*

Try this small-group activity to get your little cubs rhyming in no time! To prepare, make gameboards by placing four sticky dots on each of five index cards. Gather five students and give each child a gameboard and four bear counters. Explain that you're going to say pairs of words and want young-sters to listen for pairs that rhyme. Give youngsters the hint that each pair will contain the word *bear*. Further explain that when a player hears a rhyming pair, he should place one bear on a sticky dot on his gameboard. Then say the word *bear* and either a word that rhymes (see the list for suggestions) or one that does not. For silly fun, include some nonsense words that rhyme with *bear*. Continue playing until each player has covered all four dots. If desired, give each child a bear sticker for a job well done.

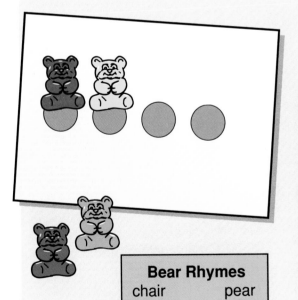

### Bear Rhymes

| | |
|---|---|
| chair | pear |
| scare | wear |
| hair | care |
| dare | fair |
| mare | rare |
| lair | |

## Big Bear, Little Bear

*Identifying and sorting uppercase and lowercase letters*

Develop awareness of uppercase and lowercase letters with this magnetic center! In advance, cut out one large bear and one small bear from tan construction paper. Tape both bears to a metal cookie sheet. Gather magnetic letters to spell bear in both all uppercase and all lowercase letters. Store the materials in a center. A child in this center identifies each letter and sorts it onto the corresponding bear. If desired, challenge the child to spell *bear* with the letters in each set.

## Hungry as a Bear

*Forming the letter B*

What's baking? Biscuits to build letter *B* awareness, of course! Gather your hungry little bear cubs and give each child a personalized five-inch square of waxed paper and a portion of refrigerated biscuit dough. Have each child roll the dough into a snake and then divide it in half. Direct her to put one half on the waxed paper. Then have her make a circle with the other half and place it on the waxed paper to complete a lowercase *B* as shown. Place each letter (still on its waxed paper square) on a cookie sheet and bake the biscuits according to the package directions. When the biscuits are cool, have each child use her finger to trace over her letter as she says, *"B* is for *bear."* Then invite her to spread her letter with butter and honey before eating. Now that's a snack any bear would be proud to devour!

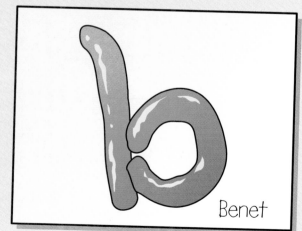

Benet

## Rhyme Time
### Matching rhymes

Someone broke all the cookies in the cookie jar! Have your little ones put the cookies back together at this rhyming center. Copy the rhyming cards on page 79. Cut them out and glue each rhyming pair onto a separate four-inch brown construction paper circle (cookie) and laminate it if desired. Use a different jigsaw-style cut on each cookie to separate the pairs. Store the cookie halves in a cookie tin and place it at a center along with a cookie sheet. A youngster removes the cookie halves, chooses one half, and names the picture. Then he finds its rhyme and places the pieced-together cookie onto the cookie sheet. He continues in this manner until each cookie is put back together. Tasty!

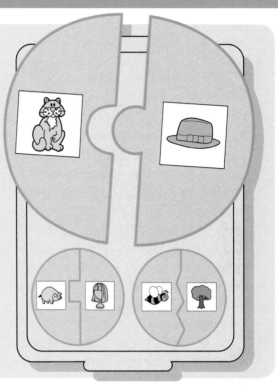

## Mark It With a Letter
### Forming letters

Your little bakers mix up a batch of letter writing skills when they create these play dough letter cookies! Provide each youngster with a small ball of play dough and a craft stick. Instruct her to flatten her play dough into a cookie shape. Lead students in the chant shown. During the chant, refer to the letter *C* on a letter chart at the appropriate verse. Then instruct each student to use her craft stick to correctly etch the letter into her cookie. Scan students' work to check for accuracy, providing help as needed. After checking their letters, have students ball up their play dough and flatten it out again. Recite the chant several times, substituting a different letter each time. To extend the activity for older students, have them form the corresponding lowercase letter in the play dough. What a great way to help your busy bakers practice forming letters!

### Pat-a-Cookie
Pat-a-cookie, pat-a-cookie,
Baker's man!
Bake us a cookie
As fast as you can.
Roll it and pat it
And mark it with a *C;*
Then there will be plenty
For you and me!

## Please Take a Cookie

### Identifying initial consonants

Use this new twist on an old classic to cook up some letter fun! To prepare, cut out a supply of three-inch brown construction paper circles to represent cookies and copy the picture cards on page 79. Cut out the cards and glue each one to a different cookie; then laminate the cookies if desired. Place the cookies in a plastic cookie jar or similar container.

Gather students in a circle and direct them to pass around the cookie jar. While passing the jar, invite youngsters to join you in reciting the chant shown. Choose a student to pick a cookie by inserting his name into the second line of the chant when he is holding the cookie jar; then have him say the third line. As the class responds with Line 4, instruct him to remove a cookie from the jar. Then have him identify the picture and say the beginning letter (or sound) in the format of the fifth line. Continue the activity in the same manner until each student has had a turn. For an added treat, pass around a cookie jar with real cookies at the conclusion of the activity!

**Class:** Please take a cookie from the cookie jar.

**Teacher:** [Child's name], take a cookie from the cookie jar.

**Student:** Who, me?

**Class:** Yes, you. What do you see?

**Student:** I see a [name of picture], and it starts with [beginning letter]!

## A Cookie Tale

### Connecting to literature, early writing

If you give a(n) _____ a cookie, he will want peanuts to go with it!

What happens when you give an elephant a cookie? This nifty project just may answer that question. Prepare a large, white paper circle with the sentence starter shown for each student. Share the book *If You Give a Mouse a Cookie* by Laura Joffe Numeroff and then enlist your students' help in generating a list of other things that go with cookies. Give each student an animal cracker and instruct her to glue it onto the first blank of the sentence starter. Then, providing help as needed, have her write an item that goes with her cookie on the second blank. Next, have her illustrate the page and glue it to a larger brown construction paper circle. Encourage students to share their stories, and then display their work on a bulletin board titled "Cookies and…"

## Sweet Sounds

*Adding onsets to rimes*

The cookie rimes at this literacy center need a dash of onsets to make them complete! To prepare, cut out 12 five-inch construction paper circles to represent cookies. Copy the picture cards on page 79 and choose 12 to use. Cut them out and glue each one to the top half of a different cookie cutout. Program the bottom half of each cookie with the word's rime, leaving a blank space for the onset. Laminate the cookies, if desired, and store them in an empty cookie tin. Place the tin at a center, along with magnetic letters and a magnetic cookie sheet. A student chooses a cookie and places it on the cookie sheet. Next, he says the name of the picture, determines the missing onset, and places the corresponding magnetic letter on the cookie to complete the word. He reads the word before removing the materials from the cookie sheet. Then he continues the activity in the same manner with the remaining cookies. Making words has never been so sweet!

## Colorful Cookie Booklets

*Identifying color words*

These personalized booklets are sure to stir up some color word practice! To prepare, cut out a 4½" x 10" brown construction paper rectangle for each student. Fold in the ends so that they meet in the middle as shown. Give each child a copy of pages 80 and 81. Read the booklet pages aloud and have each student color the pictures to match the color words in the text. Then have him cut out the pages and stack them in numerical order. Providing help as needed, have him make the body by cutting out the body part patterns and gluing them to the back of the folded brown construction paper strip. Staple the booklet pages inside of the brown construction paper. Write the title "Colorful Cookies" on the front and have each child personalize it with his name. Then invite each youngster to decorate the body as desired. After all students have completed their booklets, encourage them to read along with you and identify the color words. Yummy, yummy cookies in my tummy!

*C* is for *cookie!*

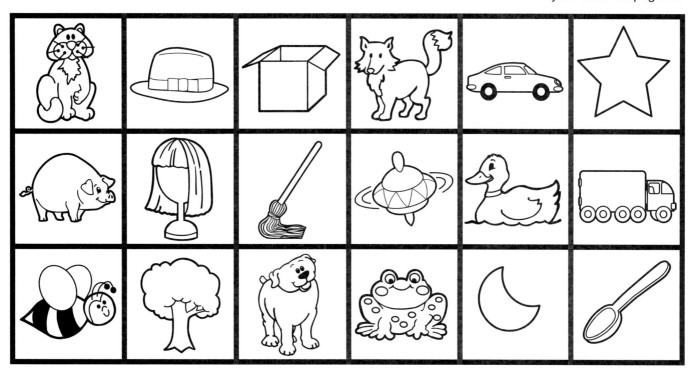

## Picture Cards
Use with "Please Take a Cookie" on page 76 and "Sweet Sounds" on page 77.

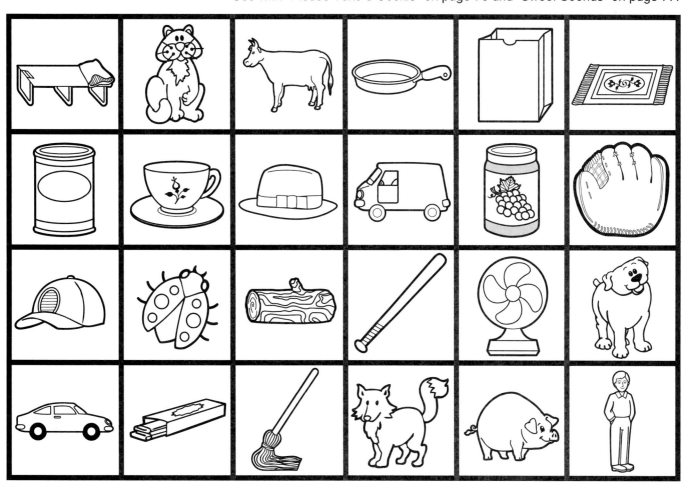

# Body Part Patterns

Use with "Colorful Cookie Booklets" on page 77.

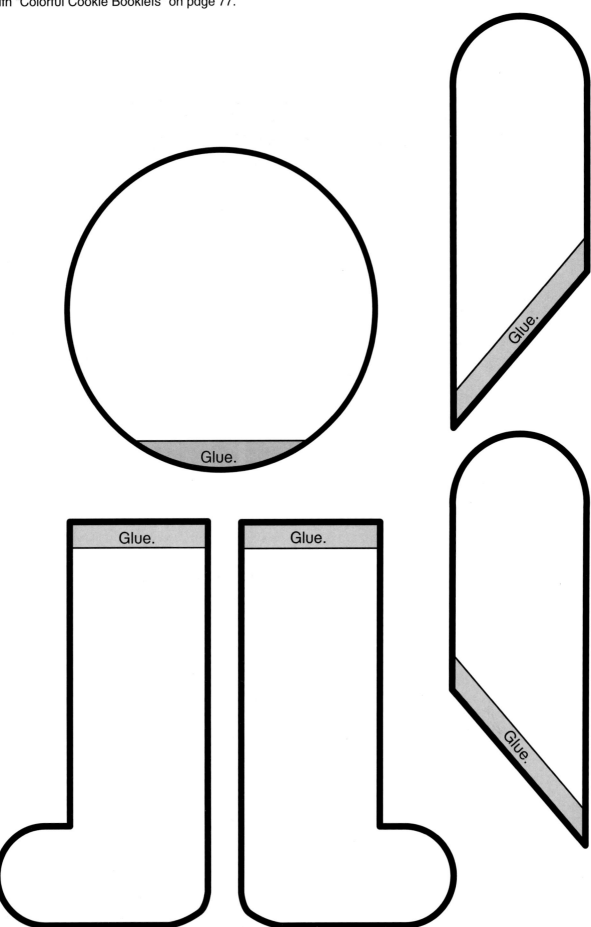

©The Mailbox® • *Simply Seasonal ABCs* • TEC60936

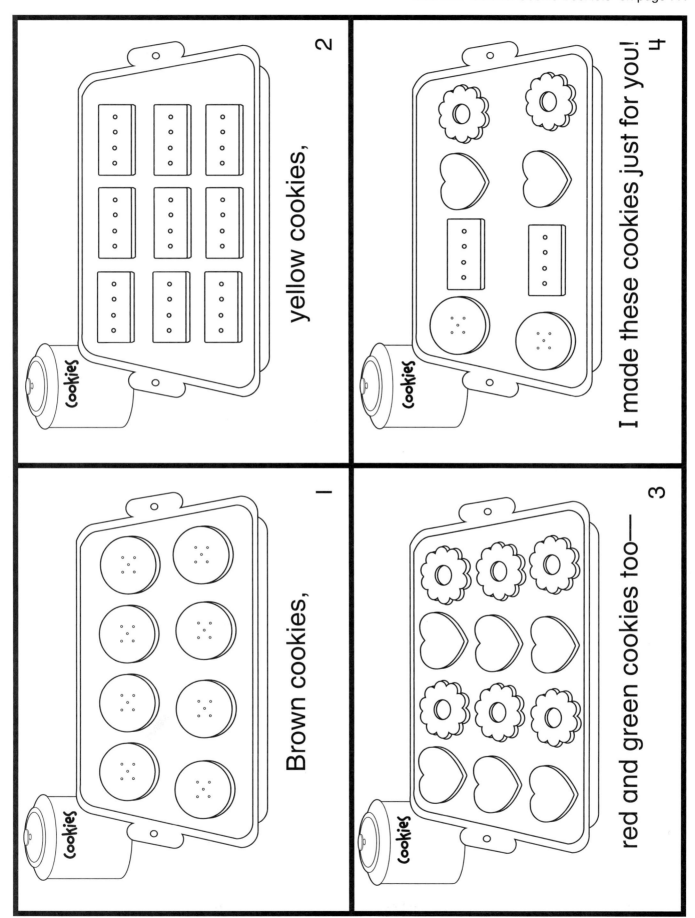

2

yellow cookies,

4

I made these cookies just for you!

1

Brown cookies,

3

red and green cookies too—

# Milk and Cookies

 Cut.

Glue the pictures that start with *C*.

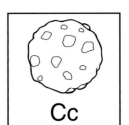
Cc

cookies

## A Valentine Vase

### *Associating V with /v/*

This V-shaped vase looks lovely holding a bouquet of valentines! Obtain three small valentines for each child. To begin, give each student a large *V* cutout and encourage him to glue it to a 12" x 18" sheet of construction paper in a contrasting color. Have each student trace the letter with his finger as he says its name. Next, have him glue three green construction paper strips (stems) inside the *V* as shown. Encourage him to glue a valentine at the top of each stem. Then have him glue green heart-shaped leaves to the stems. Explain that the words *valentine* and *vase* both begin with the letter *V*. Encourage students to say the words and exaggerate the /v/ sound. Finally, attach these lovely valentine vases to a bulletin board for a display that's simply smashing!

## Choose a Chocolate

### *Identifying initial sound /v/*

These pretend chocolates are oh so satisfying because they help youngsters learn the sound of the letter *V!* Obtain an empty heart-shaped box. Make a copy of the picture cards (page 99) on light brown construction paper to resemble chocolates. Laminate the chocolates if desired. Then place them in the box. Gather a group of youngsters. Invite a child to take a chocolate from the box. Encourage her to name the picture and then decide whether its name begins with /v/ like the word *valentine*. Continue in the same way with each remaining card, giving each child in the group at least one chance to choose a chocolate!

# Where Is Cupid?

Youngsters will have so much fun trying to find Cupid with this activity, they won't even realize they're practicing letter names! Color and cut out a copy of the cupid pattern on page 102. Place a set of alphabet cards in your pocket chart in sequential order.

Encourage students to close their eyes as you place Cupid behind a letter card. When he is securely in place, have youngsters open their eyes. Invite a student to come up to the chart, name the letter he believes Cupid is hiding behind, and then check to see whether Cupid is indeed in that location. Repeat the process until Cupid is found. When his hiding place is revealed, hide him again behind a different letter. Cupid just loves hide-and-seek!

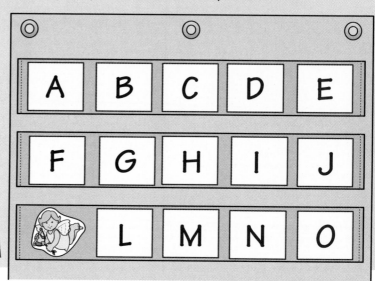

# Broken Hearts

There's no need to call a doctor—your youngsters can mend these broken hearts in a jiffy! Make a supply of red construction paper hearts. Puzzle-cut each heart to make two halves. Then label one half of each heart with a capital letter and the remaining half with the corresponding lowercase letter. Laminate the hearts for durability if desired. Then place the hearts at a center with pretend doctor items, such as a stethoscope and a lab coat. Invite a youngster to the center and encourage her to don the stethoscope and lab coat. Then have her mend the hearts by matching the uppercase and lowercase letters. That's excellent work, doctor!

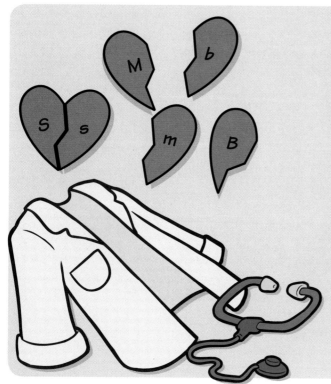

## Chant It!

### Identifying student names

Youngsters love to see their names in writing, so they're sure to be thrilled with these personalized valentines! Make a class supply of construction paper hearts. Write a different child's name on each heart. If desired, tape a Valentine's Day treat to each heart. Next, gather youngsters around and display a heart. Encourage the students to identify the name. Then recite the first two lines of the chant shown, substituting the child's name in the first line. Prompt the child whose name is on the heart to reply with the last two lines of the chant. Then encourage her to come and collect her valentine. Sweet!

[Brianna], [Brianna], do you see
A valentine to you from me?
Yes, yes, I do see
A valentine that's just for me!

## A Cookie Story

### Writing color words

Youngsters supply the color words for this vivid Valentine's Day booklet! For each child, make a copy of the booklet pages on pages 100–102. Cut out the pages, stack them in order, and staple them between two 6" x 9" covers. Use a permanent marker to label a piece of aluminum foil slightly smaller than the covers with the title shown. Give each student a booklet and have him follow along as you read each page. Instruct him to write (or dictate as you write) a different color word in each space. Then have him color the pages to reflect his chosen color words. Encourage him to write his name on the prepared foil and then glue it to the front cover to resemble a cookie sheet. Then invite him to glue a heart cutout above the title and decorate it with a variety of craft items to resemble a cookie. When the glue is dry, have each student take his booklet home to share with his family.

A Cookie Story by Josh

A Valentine cookie baked fresh today    1

sat on a counter on a _purple_ tray.    2

I added _red_ frosting    3

and _blUe_ sprinkles too.    4

It is my Valentine's Day present to you!    5

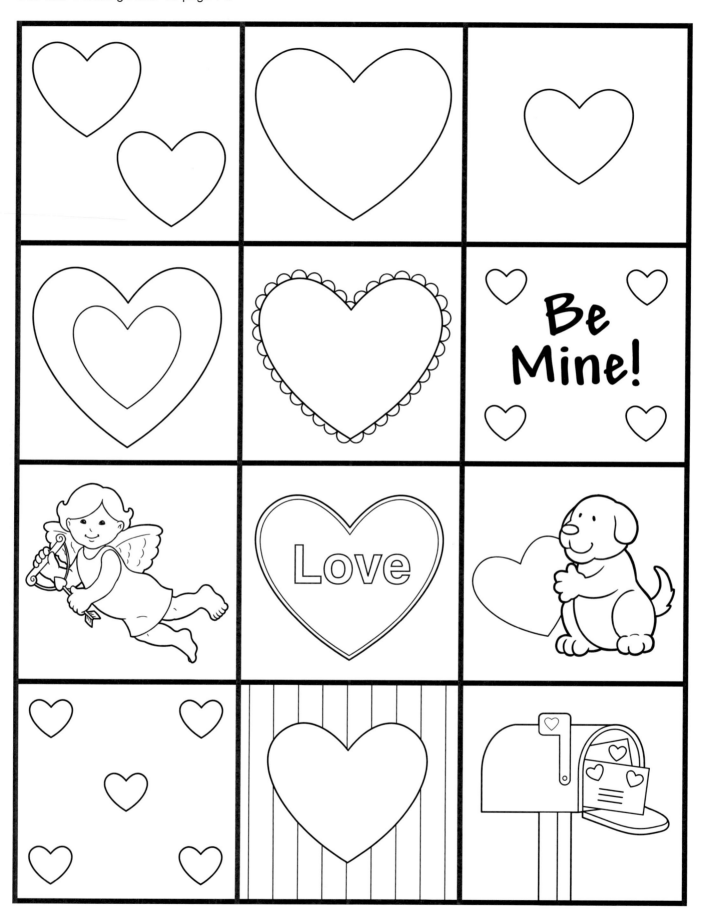

A Valentine cookie baked fresh today

1

sat on a counter on a _____ tray.

2

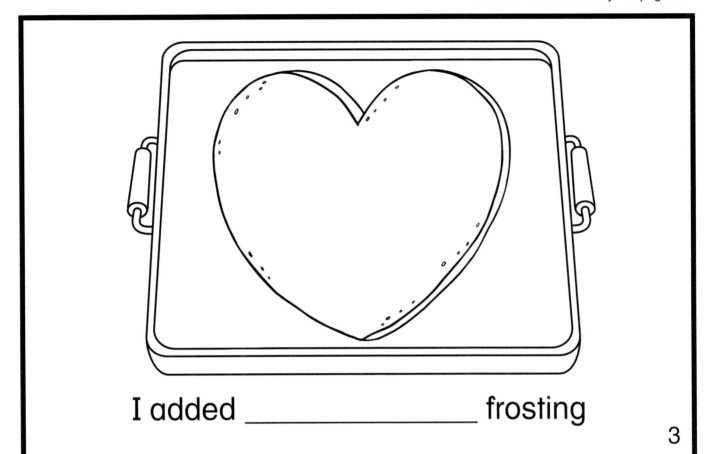

I added _____ frosting

3

and _____ sprinkles too.

4

## Booklet Page 5

Use with "A Cookie Story" on page 97.

It is my Valentine's Day present to you!

5

## Cupid Pattern

Use with "Where Is Cupid?" on page 96.

# Vv

# T Is for Teeth!

## Smiles to a T

### *Sorting pictures with the beginning sound /t/*

Watch for big smiles all around when youngsters play this small-group game. Prepare by cutting a large mouth shape from poster board. Also cut out a copy of the picture cards on page 108. Laminate the cards and the mouth for durability. Have youngsters say the word *tooth* and then identify the beginning /t/ sound. Then have one child choose a card, name the picture, and then decide whether it begins with /t/, like *tooth.* If the sounds match, he places the picture on the mouth cutout. If they do not match, he puts the card in a designated discard pile. Have youngsters take turns in this manner until all the pictures have been chosen.

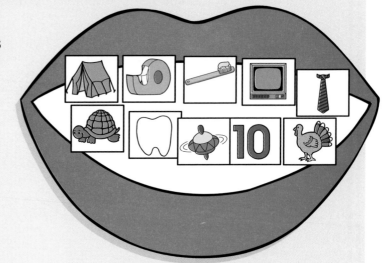

## Tic-Tac-Tooth

### *Identifying uppercase and lowercase T*

Promote phonics skills with this tooth-related twist on tic-tac-toe. Make a tooth-shaped gameboard like the one shown and laminate it for durability. Collect a supply of plastic milk jug caps. Use a permanent marker to program one set of caps with an uppercase *T* and another set with a lowercase *T.* Invite partners to sort the caps into two separate piles (uppercase and lowercase) and have each child take one set of caps. Then help youngsters play the game. Tic-tac-tooth!

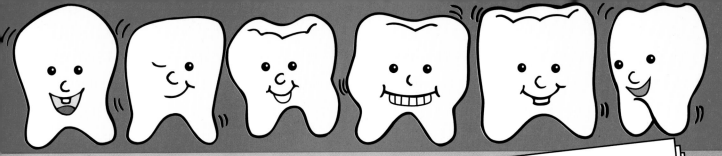

## Careful Treatment

### Recognizing initial consonants

Clean teeth are happy teeth! Reinforce the importance of taking care of teeth as youngsters create this letter identification booklet. Give each child a copy of pages 109 and 110. Read the text aloud. Have her trace each uppercase letter and circle the corresponding lowercase letter in the sentence. Ask her to personalize her cover and then color the cover and booklet pages. Next, help her cut out the cover and each booklet page and the corresponding pattern. Have her glue each pattern in the space provided. Help her sequence the booklet pages behind the cover and staple it together along the left side. Then invite partners to read their booklets to each other.

## Loose Tooth

### Promoting language and listening skills

Get the wiggles out as youngsters perform this action rhyme. Teach students the provided rhyme. Next, divide youngsters into four groups and assign each group one of the first four lines of the rhyme. Have the students in each group say their group's line as they wiggle the corresponding body part. Then have everyone repeat the last two lines as they pretend to wiggle a tooth.

> I wiggled my fingers.
> I wiggled my toes.
> I wiggled my ears.
> I wiggled my nose.
> I wiggled my tooth,
> Just the same.
> I wiggled and wiggled,
> And out it came!

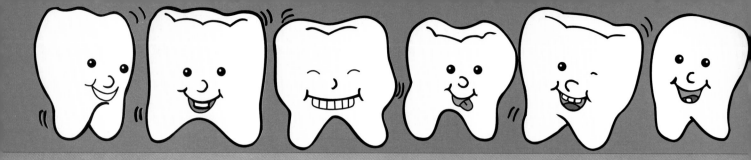

## Toothy Grins

**Using left-to-right progression**

Pearly whites shine all around with these toothy self-portraits! Cut out several tooth-shaped sponges and then hot-glue each sponge onto a film canister as shown. Program a sheet of paper with a large head and mouth shape as shown. Make a skin-toned construction paper copy for each child plus one extra copy for yourself. Give each child a sheet and have him use crayons to draw facial features to make the face resemble his own. Tell young-sters that when writing or reading, they work from left to right. Next, model for youngsters how to dip a sponge into a shallow container of white paint and print a row of teeth, working from left to right. Invite each child to copy the process to print two rows of teeth on the mouth of his self-portrait. When the paint is dry, cut out each self-portrait and display the smiles for all to see.

## Terrific Twenty

**Naming words that begin with /t/**

Teach youngsters that they have 20 tiny teeth with this phonemic awareness activity. Make a mouth shape on a large piece of red poster board as shown (or use the gameboard from "Smiles to a T" on page 104). Place 20 white DUPLO blocks (teeth) in a pillowcase. Gather youngsters in a circle around the mouth shape and tell

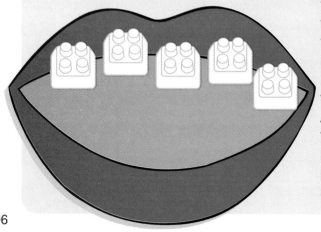

them they are going to fill it with 20 teeth to match the number of their baby teeth. Ask them to name the beginning sound they hear in the word *tooth* and then guide the group to say "*T,* tooth, /t/." Pass the bag to a child and have her draw one tooth and then name something that begins with /t/. If she is correct, have her place the tooth on the mouth cutout. If she is not correct, have her place the tooth back in the bag. Then have her pass the bag to another child and repeat the activity.

106

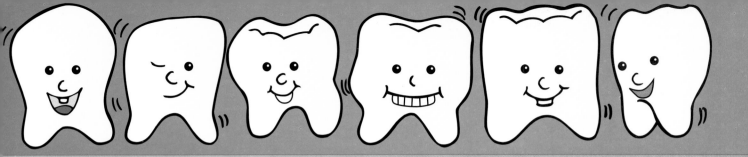

## Tooth Fairy Troubles
### Writing to complete a sentence

Does the tooth fairy ever mix up little ones' teeth? Youngsters discover the answer when you share the story *Nice Try, Tooth Fairy* by Mary W. Olson. Discuss with students how the tooth fairy tries several times to find the correct tooth but each time delivers a different animal's tooth to the little girl. Then give each child a sheet programmed with the sentence starter shown. Encourage each youngster to think about the animals in the story and then help her write to complete the sentence using a different animal name. Then, have her illustrate her sentence. After each child shares her work with the class, bind the pages together with a student-made cover to make a class book.

The tooth fairy brought a
*tigrs tooth!*

## Brushing Up!
### Adding onsets to rimes

Brush up on word family skills with this partner activity. Make two copies of the toothbrush handle and several copies of the toothbrush head (patterns below). Program each toothbrush handle with a different rime and each toothbrush head with an onset to form word family words. Laminate the patterns for durability. Partner 1 forms a word with a chosen onset and rime and then reads it aloud with your help as needed. Then Partner 2 takes a turn, and they continue in the same manner as time allows.

## Toothbrush Patterns
Use with "Brushing Up!" on this page.

©The Mailbox® • *Simply Seasonal ABCs* • TEC60936

# T is for teeth!

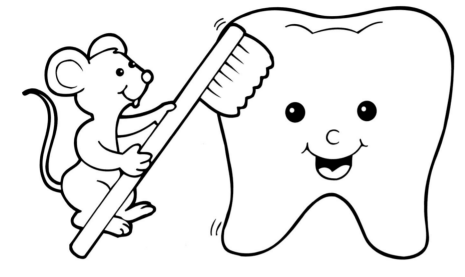

Name _____

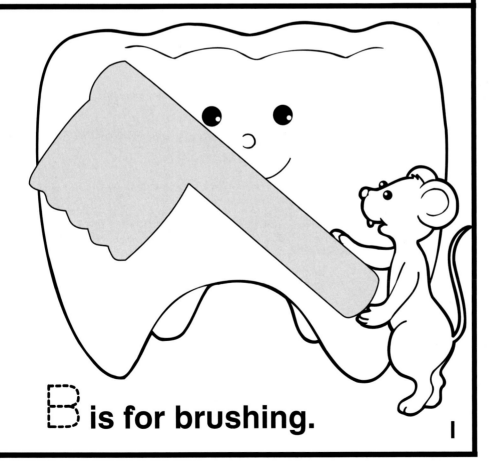

# B is for brushing.

1

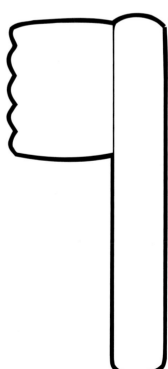

F is for flossing.

2

Floss

S is for smiling.

3

# Toothy Critters

 Color. 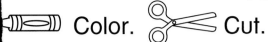 Cut.

 Name each animal.

Glue the beginning sound.

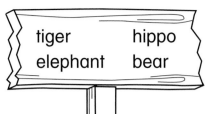

tiger     hippo

elephant    bear

T t E e H h B b

# Tt